WHAT MAKES IT GO?

Written by Rod Barkman

MOTORCYCLES

Enslow PUBLISHING

Published in 2027 by Enslow Publishing, LLC
2544 Clinton Street
Buffalo, NY 14224

Written by: Rod Barkman
Edited by: Beth Latham
Designed by: Dan Scase

Cataloging-in-Publication Data

Names: Barkman, Rod.
Title: Motorcycles / Rod Barkman.
Description: Buffalo, NY : Enslow Publishing, 2027. | Series: What makes it go? | Includes glossary and index.
Identifiers: ISBN 9781978548244 (pbk.) | ISBN 9781978548251 (library bound) | ISBN 9781978548268 (ebook)
Subjects: LCSH: Motorcycles--Juvenile literature.
Classification: LCC TL440.15 B375 2027 | DDC 629.2275--dc23

Printed in China

CPSIA compliance information: Batch #QS27ENS: For further information contact Enslow Publishing LLC, New York, New York at 1-800-398-2504.

Please visit our website, www.enslowpublishing.com. For a free color catalog of all our high-quality books, call toll free 1-800-398-2504 or fax 1-877-980-4454.

Find us on

Image Credits

Images courtesy of Shutterstock.com, unless otherwise stated.

Cover and Recurring – Donglpix, Jakub Sisulak. 2–3 – Lukas Gojda. 4–5 – Audio und werbung, Jakub Sisulak. 6–7 – Melnikov Dmitriy, Hafiz Johari. 8–9 – Jakub Sisulak, andreonegin, Everyonephoto Studio, konstantinos69. 10–11 – DmyTo, Nikkolia. 12–13 – Eugene Ga, HY-DP. 14–15 – Armensl, REDCHYTS FEDIR. 16–17 – Lukas Gojda, oceanjohn. 18–19 – Snapstitch Photography, Audio und werbung. 20–21 – Boyloso, Fenix Prods. 22–23 – CC7, Kitreel.

CONTENTS

WORDS THAT LOOK LIKE THIS CAN BE FOUND IN THE GLOSSARY ON PAGE 24.

WHAT IS A MOTORCYCLE?

A motorcycle is a vehicle that has two wheels. An engine gives the motorcycle the power to move forward. A motorcycle can carry up to two people.

Would you like to ride a motorcycle?

A person on a motorcycle is called a rider. The rider uses the handlebars to steer. There are different parts to a motorcycle.

MOTORCYCLES IN EVERYDAY LIFE

People ride motorcycles to get themselves to all kinds of places, such as work. Motorcycles are also used by delivery drivers. They are often used when delivering small things, such as fast food.

Lots of people ride motorcycles for fun around cities and in the country. Motorcycles are also used in sports. Some motorcycle racing takes place on a tarmac track. Other motorcycles race on mud and dirt.

Motorcycle racing is a dangerous sport.

TYPES OF MOTORCYCLES

There are many types of motorcycles. How many of these have you seen?

Sport motorcycles are the fastest types of bikes. They are light and built for racing.

Off-road motorcycles are not meant to be driven on roads. Instead, they go on dirt, mud, or gravel.

Touring motorcycles are large and comfortable. They are made to go long distances on roads.

Street motorcycles are simple, light, and easy to use. They are made for riding around a city.

Scooters have small wheels and are easy to control. They are made to be comfortable.

CUSTOM BIKES

Lots of riders add, change, or take away parts of their motorcycles. Motorcycles that have been changed in this way are called custom bikes. A chopper is a famous type of custom bike.

Bobbers are another well-known type of custom bike. A bobber is a type of custom bike where many parts have been taken away to make the motorcycle faster.

These are cafe racers, which are custom bikes for racing on roads.

MOTORCYCLE CONTROLS

The rider turns the throttle to make the motorcycle go faster. The throttle is on the right handlebar. The headlight, horn, and blinkers are controlled by buttons, which are usually on the left handlebar.

Instruments are in the middle of the handlebars. These show important things, such as how fast the bike is going.

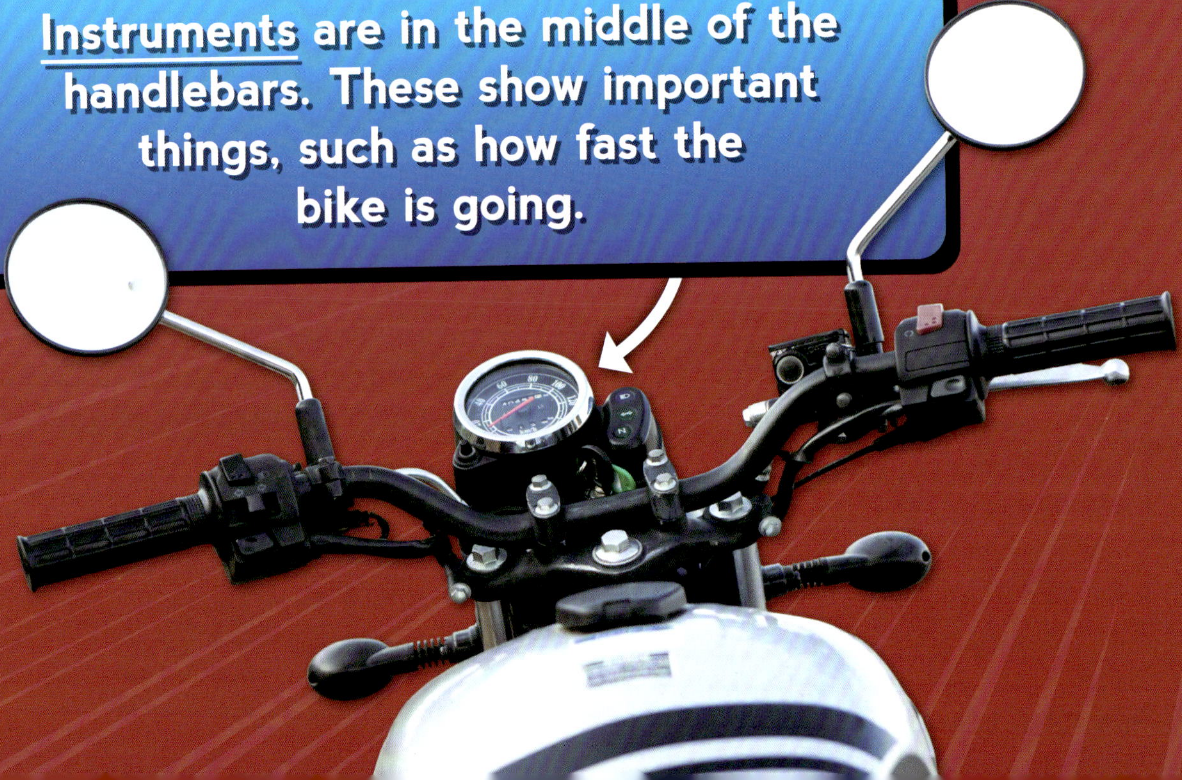

The brakes slow the motorcycle down. The brake for the front wheel is controlled with a lever by the handlebar. The brake for the back wheel is usually controlled by a pedal under the rider's right foot.

To steer, the rider uses the handlebars and also leans in the direction they want to go.

HISTORY

The first vehicle to have two wheels and an engine powered by gas was invented in Germany in the 1800s. Many people think this was the first motorcycle. It was built by a man called Gottlieb Daimler.

This is what Daimler's first motorcycle would have looked like.

A sidecar is something that a passenger can ride in. It can be attached to a bike. Sidecars were first invented for bicycles in the 1800s. In the 1900s, they were made for motorcycles too.

HOW DO MOTORCYCLES STAY UP?

When a motorcycle moves, it sometimes leans to one side or the other. To stop the bike from falling over, the rider will lean in the same direction that the motorcycle is wobbling.

This small lean from the rider moves the wheels back underneath the motorcycle. This means that the motorcycle stays balanced and remains upright. The rider often does this without thinking about it.

The wheels, steering, and handlebars of bikes are cleverly built to keep them balanced.

SCIENCE OF MOTORCYCLES

A motorcycle pushes through the air as it moves. This slows the motorcycle down, which is called drag. Motorcycles that have a smoother, pointier shape move through the air more easily. This means less drag.

Less drag makes a motorcycle faster and easier to control.

Fairings are the panels that cover the frame and engine of a motorcycle. Fairings make the whole bike smoother, which deflects the air around the bike. A windshield helps push air around the rider too.

Riders must make themselves as small as possible when going fast.

SAFETY

Motorcycle helmets have three layers. The outer layer is often made of a hard type of plastic. The middle layer cushions the person's head in a crash. The last layer is soft to make the helmet comfortable.

Wearing a helmet is one of the most important ways to stay safe on a motorcycle.

Protective clothing can also help keep riders safe. There are jackets, boots, gloves, and pants specially made for riding motorcycles. Some clothing is brightly colored and reflects light. This makes riders easier for other drivers to see.

THE FUTURE

Most motorcycle engines are powered with gas. However, using gas harms the planet. Electric motorcycles are much better, as long as the electricity comes from renewable energy sources. In the future, many motorcycles might be electric.

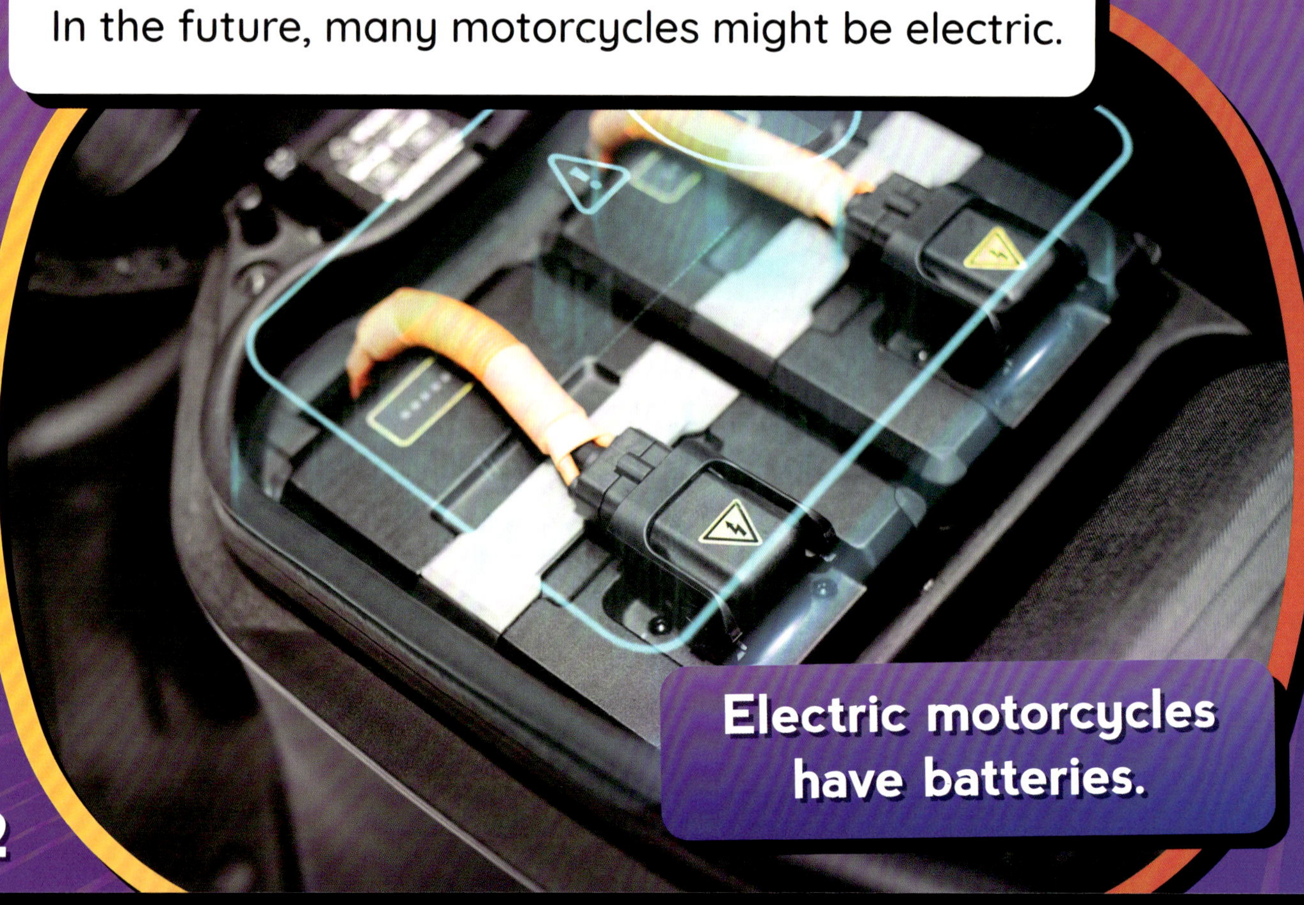

Electric motorcycles have batteries.

Future motorcycle helmets may have cameras fixed to the back and a see-through screen built into the visor. The screen would show what is behind the rider, as well as maps and other information.

Now you've learned about motorcycles, what do you think they will look like in the future?

GLOSSARY

blinkers small flashing lights on the side of a vehicle that can be turned on to show other drivers which way it is about to go when it turns

deflects makes something change its direction

gas a kind of oil used as fuel to make some engines work

instruments devices used to measure things, such as speed and height

passenger a person who is carried in or on something that is moving

renewable energy power made from sources that do not run out, such as wind or solar energy

tarmac a material made of stones and tar, used to make roads

visor the moveable part of a helmet that is pulled down in front of the eyes

INDEX